THROWBACKS

Spinner Publications, Inc.
164 William Street
New Bedford, Massachusetts 02740

Design: Jay Avila
Cover photograph: John K. Robson

Library of Congress Cataloging-in-Publication Data

Bobrick, James, 1942-
  Throwbacks : selected poems / by James Bobrick.
    p. cm.
  ISBN 0-932027-96-2 (pbk.)
  1. Title.

PS3602.027T49 2005
811'.6--dc22   2005029541

THROWBACKS
SELECTED POEMS

JAMES BOBRICK

Spinner Publications, Inc.

New Bedford, Massachusetts

For Gloria
and
For Sebastian and Miranda

Acknowledgments

"Valentine" first appeared in *Candelabrum Poetry Magazine*;
"Shave" in *Cumberland Poetry Review*; "Premature Labor"
in *The Eclectic Muse*; "At Fresh Pond Plaza" in *Four I's*;
"Another Nineties, New Bedford" "Swain School of Design
1881–1988" and "Lines for Mike" in *Lactuca*; "Jury Duty" in
Laurel Review; "Cheap Date" in *Oval Magazine*; "Trip" in *The
Neovictorian*; "Job Hunting" in *the new renaissance*; "Life's a
Beach" in *Newport Review*; "Exhibition" and "Castaway" in
Northeast Journal; "Bank" in *Oxford Magazine*; "Coding Out"
"Senex Amator" and "Song for an Old Mattress" in *Parting
Gifts*; "Canto Populare" in *Penny Dreadful Review*; "Conte" in
Poetry Motel; "Enjambment" in *The Press of the Third Mind*;
"Extraction" in *Rattle*; "Early Show" in *Slant*; "Throwbacks"
in *South Coast Poetry Journal*; "Answering Machine" in
Troubadour; "Tattoo" in *Tucumcari Literary Review*; "Overcoat"
in *Visions International*; "Olympia Market, New Bedford"
in *Worcester Review*; "Wake Up Call" in *Writer's Journal*;
"Kingdom Come" in *Yet Another Small Magazine*.

The author wishes to thank the University of Massachusetts
Dartmouth for a grant toward the publication of this book.

CONTENTS

1

THROWBACKS

Strange to see how
on side streets or
unlikely corners
in Chelsea some
old newsstands—green,
wooden, the kind

that padlock like
toolsheds—survive,
dubious pre-
McLuhan structures
whose owners still
live strictly by

the daily papers'
horology—
opening early
then shut until
rush hour arrives
below Penn Station.

All that time spent
sitting in dark
cramped cells, a living?
Rather a sort
of charity
when being there

gives back less cost-
effective days
from relics left
like paperweights
on what's recalled
of neighborhoods.

JURY DUTY

First range-finding forms, leaving smudges of carbon,
then point-blank summons—
the law always has you dead to rights;
tracks, locks on, adjusts its sights.

The orientation officer doesn't bother with his holster.
A judge admonishes from dual monitors
in black and white, mouth a sad oval.
Penalties for bolting are vague but real.

Each windowless courtroom differs
only in latticework laid over
the single huge light-diffusion disc in the ceiling,
dizzying overlays—grille, circle, grid, mesh—

some minimalist Piranesi perhaps
collaborating on the design
like those masters on the roofs of cathedrals
who sculpted for God's eyes.

SENEX AMATOR

"Love is a kiss, necessity a knot"
of drugs and meds and florid syndromes—pot,
Ecstasy, Deprenyl, Clonazepam…
it gets old, acting younger than I am,
like always being on and on the spot.

What hit made *Dexy's Midnight Runners* hot?
The factoids thirty-somethings haven't forgot
mean fifty-somethings bomb, for all they cram.
     Love is a kiss,

and, broken off, the self-destructive plot
is set in motion: better, better not
inflict sick fancies like Miss Havisham,
enter a monastery and make jam;
I've traded years for days. Now it's all shot.
     Love is a kiss.

CODING OUT
(in memory of Leo Kelley)

Intensive chemo as a last resort
but no remission. Tubed, drugged, mute, you lay
curled to your johnny's length on life support.
While you could use a pad, scrawls left for me
resolved to reading lists for liberal arts
(which we both taught), a weird six-figure price
beside each item. I'm going to say
those twisted digits, skewed through circuitry
gone haywire, functioning by fits and starts,
signaled a poet's love for what's precise.

There were more trendy ironies as well:
the cancer ward whose layout and décor
flaunted its tacky past as a motel;
young social workers stopping by to tweak
clichés from Kübler-Ross; nurses in smart
new outfits and designer duty shoes,
interns with tailored lab coats, models for
the fashion statement hyped as "scrub suit chic";
specialists scribbled orders, read a chart,
then pulled away in BMWs.

Ridged swellings shaped like muttonchops appeared,
the sharp blocks in the throat. I'd gone numb, though
a day's growth brought out bald spots in my beard
as big as quarters. On that last night there
beside you, respirator gasping, I
pondered a poster of Mt. Everest,
"Roof of the World," a friend had taped up—snow,
rocks, nodes of cloud mass, bands of thinning air,
ice-blue, blue-black, then higher pitch-dark sky—
breath crushed under the pack years in my chest.

ANOTHER NINETIES, NEW BEDFORD

"The gorgeous iridescence of decay."
Not even close. A grubby vestibule
flanked by the landlord's beauty parlor—cracked
plate glass, bleached stills, lopsided spider plants
trailing exhausted runners; in the back
two cramped apartments, mine a factory-green
half-basement, lit by skylights, countersunk
six feet below the ground. Buried alive!
For a while I saw myself living out
a part made up of *Notes From Underground*,
Là-Bas, Strindberg's cloacal hell... as if
outer and inner really did adhere
like those old-fashioned vacuum hemispheres.
It soon grew harder to romanticize
the August heat and smell of garbage mixed
with rotten eggs after a run of perms.
Would "monochrome marcescence" be more apt?
I wondered if the other tenant, old
Cabral, had felt some grand symbolic role
dwindle to a B-movie's wooden props,
his dark suit and fedora? The first time
we ever met, out of the blue he said,
"Every night I make it stiff, this I mean,"
giving his brim a studied tug. "You start
by rubbing it with chalk and vaseline."

LINES FOR MIKE

Out of high school too late for
Korea, after a hitch
you took classes off and on,
sweetly beat, always reading,
the mind's *wanderjahr* prolonged
through those still literate years,
the GI Bill's silver age.
Hip romantic who tutored
dropouts gratis and laughed off
an ex-girlfriend's scheme to set
you up as a gigolo—
"Dr. Mike's meat injection
isn't available on
the commodities market."

Berkeley was where it was at;
your picture appeared in *Life*,
one of a group confronting
General Maxwell Taylor.
Then drugs. One day someone pulled
a gun; you saw yourself (out-
of-body experience)
a sack on the pavement and
faded into the Cascades,
old parachute for a tent,
to crash a decade later
back in Cambridge, in the same
house where you'd been raised, now an
outpatient facility.

"'Unreal city.' Everyone
 I grew up with," you added,
"is either a cop or dead."
Some idiosyncratic
macrobiotics, mostly
former heads, offered shelter.
Rice and TM helped until
one of them was diagnosed
with stomach cancer despite
daily megadoses of
vitamin C. You began
drinking gallons of water
to flush the poisons, became
scarily thin with metal
breath and tapioca skin.

They found your body one night
(starvation later given
as the official cause) where
the railroad tracks cut across
Mass. Ave. near the river, where
the roadbed running west through
the green tunnel of summer
past weathered improbable
boxcars left on a siding—
Canadian Pacific,
Great Northern—makes it seem more
like Ogallala than just
a few blocks from MIT.

I remember you said that
in the forties, growing up,
the railroad was the frontier,
your turf's boundary. A gang of
black kids, headhunters it was
rumored, hung out up the tracks;
for a long time you never
dared to venture beyond them.

THE SKAIAN GATES
(from the Iliad Book XXII)

Dog days, heat fracturing the scorched earth,
with Sirius rising, disastrous star,
livid and brilliant, a red warning hung
far through stupendous arcades of starlight
when fevers rage and men begin to die.
So, on the plain, Achilleus' breastplate shone.

... Hektor stood silent, aloof
and didn't budge an inch. Propped on his spear
he scanned the plain, eyes glinting like mica,
tautened like a diamondback rattlesnake
coiled by its hole in the lonely foothills,
mean, peevish, turgid with venom, tickering
irritably as some careless hunter
comes crashing towards it through the underbrush.
So Hektor waited, pondering alone.

And Hektor lay there, babbling blood,
chest heaving; breathing was like lifting weights.
He tried to speak and choked and tried again.
"I beg you,...by your father...by your knees,
honor the gods and give my body back.
Your time is coming, coming soon. I see
Death and Apollo smiling to themselves
as Paris' sizzling arrow bites your heel."
His life hissed through the fissures of his teeth
and faded like a breath in frosty air.

Achilleus yanked out his spear and said, "Die
and they, they can do what they like to me."

EQUINOXES

Summer is over. From the tip
of the fountain's still sunlit stem
the petals of water flower
and scatter; the failing shower
beats out its humdrum requiem
against the broken basin. Drip

by drip the splits widen, the lime-
stone dissolves, trickles through the drains:
I time my heart's stammer and thud.
The slow erosion of the blood
laboring up and down my veins
repeats the tired pantomime.

II

Once more in Aries day and night
the sun and clearest constellations shed
the eastern Garden's priscal light

on punished flesh the sweetness gathers back,
as you, spring's sigil in its stead,
climb to the flashpoint of the zodiac.

EARLY SHOW

Semi-private screening at the multiplex—
two old ladies down in front,
yaffling about *The Madness of King George*
and us, in the back row, mad for sex.

Lights dim. You scrump my chest hair,
I coax wetness through your jeans,
playing tonsil hockey's glottal stops....
Now and then I glimpse, coming up for air,

the asylum's enlightened cruelties
Rx for the king, who, it would appear,
comes to his senses by reading (guess what?) *Lear.*
From this trendy costume drama,

accessories by Foucault,
I recall two lines, the first because you laughed,
my stagy "best film I've ever seen,"
your "I want you so."

PREMATURE LABOR

The digital display
would uptick, speed up, blur,
read out then ebb away,
idling on the monitor.
Contractions came each day.

The pregnant womb, once said
to mirror the heavens and earth,
now calls to mind instead
how tides that move toward birth
can cast us up stone dead,

tugged by receding galaxies....
What good was your daily rate
of growth by slow degrees,
each fifteen grams' makeweight,
placed in the scales with these?

Still nine weeks to get through—
they had to intervene
when water broke, so you
were laid out, wrapped, washed clean,
then (presto) as if on cue

the nurse, magician-style,
palmed back the oxyhood:
there! breathing freely—while
in an eyelid's curve I could
trace an archaic smile.

CANTO POPULARE

(after the Italian)

The Saracens adore the sun
and Turks the moon and stars, while I
your hair's to-die-for highlights set on high.

Sailors will call on all their saints
for succor when about to drown;
you're all that fills my mouth as I go down.

Each slave craves some way to escape
and break the bondage of his chains—
from you I crave what binds me and restrains.

SWAIN SCHOOL OF DESIGN 1881–1988

Columns and railings flake, hedges shag. Weeds
kick up the parking lot and rank lawns beneath
the chestnut blossoms' listing chandelier.

Boarded up nearly a year this May, the campus
composes itself as for a series of plates—
Old Views of County Street, Lost New Bedford —

drug on the market, Greek Revival folly,
while realtor and developer finesse
variances for condos, offices.

"Craft of eye and hand and imagination,"
same old story...but now something smoldering, drawn
through the hubble-bubble of recollection,

calls up among cloudy figures one Ibrahim Pasha,
his grief at the mosques of Belgrade turned into barracks,
baths into stables, homes into brothels and taverns.

JOB HUNTING

Although he'd tried to empty
himself—going several times
at home and twice in the bus
terminal before the hour's
ride to the big interview,
not having coffee and just
rinsing his mouth with water
once—after a few minutes
distending tenderness saw
him squeezed into the restroom
at the rear, lifting the seat
and looking down a bottomless
Day-Glo orange bucket set
flush with vaguely beige plastic
at turquoise froth that sloshed and
seethed chemically below.
He canted stiffly forward,
left arm extended, clutching
the handgrip, knees locked to brace
his frame against the bus'
juddering while at the same time
his right hand tilted to arc
the weak steam safely away
from his pants; but half gagging
on a bubble gum updraft
of disinfectant, he tucked
in too soon (hysteresis
palpable) drops oozing through
the tan featherweight fabric
so that later, it appeared,
one of the interviewers
focused exclusively on
a marginally darker
area beside his fly.
Another example of
the "physopathology
of everyday life," *nicht wahr?*

CONTE

Ms. Junior Faculty grown paranoid
dumps older colleague who lacks power base.
She's up for tenure. Note the commonplace
of academic fiction here deployed,

and this concinnity: she turns him in
along with final grades and incompletes.
Late June. He comes upon old T-shirt sheets,
her hand-me-downs, sage-colored and worn thin.

Stretched on the mattress every stain and spot
is scrutinized intently like a slide;
kiwi cross sections, kanji magnified
are porn as stylized as the money shot.

Some boyfriend has her prone, pinned to the bed,
cock like a handle works her pubic hair,
sex finding its abstract expression there
in fluid brushstrokes. Zoom out. Now, instead,

he sees himself, viewed from a growing height,
shrink and dissolve, sheets widening like a pond,
adrift like Thumbelina, but beyond
the range of fairy tale and rescue flight.

Life's a Beach

Afternoons down along the shore
you appear around five, slick fashion plate—
J. Press, J. Crew, some upscale store.

Then starting from the bottom line of foam
where waves break and de-escalate,
falling risers flattening to a comb,

you zigzag slowly up the sand,
clutching a plastic scoop with built-in sieve,
metal detector dowsing and

waved over stog and litter like a fan.
Have margins narrowed that you live
on windfalls from each bottle, coin, or can?

Roads to Fatima

*The famous pilgrimage town where three peasant children
claimed to have seen the "Virgin of the Rosary" on 13 May 1917 and
again on the 13th of each subsequent month until October in that
year.... On the far side of the esplanade rises the gigantic basilica,
flanked by colonnades.*

                                      –Baedeker's Portugal

Around the clock the second week
in August, they straggled along National One
through smog from traffic, nearby
wild fires. Record heat was reaching its peak.

Your mother's guestroom nudged the highway's shoulder.
One night some pilgrims paused just outside;
through the open window Portuguese
sampled our pants and obscenities,

"Latin's last flower," your native language, plucked
(it fevered me to think) as we fucked.
Get real, I told myself later, trying
to picture you in fascism's '50s time warp:

a third world child who tended sheep and
played house, using the silvery undersides
of olive leaves as sardines, for whom, innocent
of utilities, Fatima was Disneyland.

Begun the same year as the dictatorship,
this budget St. Peter's, blown up photos
of the three children now collaged to its facade,
reads on the literal level as pure kitsch.

Afterwards, killing time in the bus station,
I wiggled double-image postcards back and forth:
Jesus/Sacred Heart, Basilica/Paschal Lamb—revelation
is unique, its flip sides much the same.

Enjambment

1990

February 21	–Frank Currier died
August 5	–Anne Bennett died
August 11	–Aunt Emma operated on
September 3	–Uncle John taken sick and went to hospital
October 8	–Uncle John had another coronary
November 6	–Mr. Lane died
November 23	–Aunt Grace operated on
November 27	–Walter Wilton died
November 30	–Sonny Downer died
December 24	–Dad had gall bladder attack

1991

January 14	–Uncle John died
February 11	–Mom operated on
March 6	–Evelyn died
March 31	–Dad had second gall bladder attack
April 2	–Dad operated on (gall bladder)
June 4	–Mr. Laubinger died
July 19	–Tobey hit by car
October 18	–Aunt Emma died
November 4	–Ralph Gordon died
December 18	–Dad operated on for prostate
December 30	–Al Poole had coronary

1992

January 24	-Al Poole died
January 27	-Dave operated on
March 3	-Aunt Sadie had heart attack
March 5	-Aunt Sadie died
August 10	-Mom had lump removed
August 17	-Gram Currier died
August 19	-Mom operated on
September 2	-Tony Mondoono died
September 5	-I had tooth out
September 7	-Dad went for blood transfusions
October 3	-Dad went for blood transfusions
November 29	-Dad died
December 30	-Mom went to Mt. Auburn

1993

January 6	-Mom operated on for leg trouble
May 2	-I was operated on for gall bladder
May 17	-Trixie died
June 26	-Got Candy (garage sale)
August 10	-Aunt Ollie died
August 25	-JJC had wart removed
September 4	-Mom went to hospital for tests

1994

January 14	-Mom went to Mt. Auburn, possible coronary
February 9	-I discovered I had high blood pressure
March 27	-Mom went to Mt. Auburn in ambulance
April 2	-Mom operated on to put pin in her left hip
April 28	-Mom transferred to rehab center
June 2	-Mom passed away

2

KINGDOM COME

In third grade I
longed to be Catholic—
early release
for catechism,
passes to *Quo*
Vadis, because

a friend said darkly,
"we go to heaven
when we die," crossing
himself, house dealer's
assured blur, in-
imitable

despite hours of
mirrored practice.
But most of all
I coveted
the medalled chains,
cords, crucifixes,

Christophers, horn-like
squiggles—survival's
hard currency.
Russia had gotten
the Bomb. Drills were
frequent. We filed

into the cloakroom
or crouched under
desks, covering
up with thin arms.
Soon ID bracelets
were issued. On

the pretext that,
my head blown off,
who I was wouldn't
matter, I wore
the engraved plate
around my neck.

EXHIBITION

Love's declension: yes, why, if only, free.
March, April, May…regression, tantrums, pain.
Instead of letting go I tried to drain
the drying tit of Roman Charity.

June. Record crowds pushed through the MFA.
You'd gone with someone younger so I thought
that's that, till to the life I saw you caught
inside on that mosaic from Pompeii.

Afterward it seemed plastered every place
in Boston—tesserae like microdots
blown up on posters less to publicize

than steal the show—same wistful, flower child's face,
pieced out in ochers and forget-me-nots,
Venus Pandemos smiling in the eyes.

BLOCKS

I'm somewhere between flaneur
and failure, he thought, weighing
and discarding phrases as
he walked east on 14th Street,
sorting like a bag lady
through the jumble of causes
for what he now chose to term
"syntagmatic graphasia,"
viz. the chronic problem of
not being able to put
words together on paper
despite the obsessive need
to try which remained and racked
him with dry sporadic heaves.
When he reached for his memo
book, as he still at times did,
to keep from feeding at least
a few of his fragments to
the mental shredder, mental
shredder? this time the gesture,
catching him off guard, brought back
the way he used to carry
a pocket *Fleurs du Mal*, bought
that distant summer before
college from a dealer in
foreign books in a narrow
dusty overcrowded room
three flights up with tall ladders
on slide rails; brought back how the
rot-and-schlock-transfiguring
lines gave him a rush, a flash
of images for poems he
planned to write, whose promise cast
rancid glamor on these streets.
At that the wasted years' raw

sewage backed up in his throat,
so he sought distraction in
a porno theater, its
binary oppositions,
the task of telling real sex
sounds from fake, noticing too
late the film was an import
which meant, of course—On the screen
the raucously dubbed fucking
continued, new pair, same track.

VALENTINE

*Dartmouth, an extensive oceanfront town south and west of New
Bedford, offers numerous back roads. The landscape is flat with
broad stretches of farmland and salt marshes.*

Dusk. Cold. Half-hidden, we park—lovers crossed
by passing headlights, though things uttered through
raw need, translated and condensed, soon print
out on closed windows their protective tint
that deepens to tones mixed like Pentecost,
tongues speaking wildly what they've wanted to.

At last the head and windshield start to clear;
trees spin more slowly round us in a ring,
rising and falling, shudder and then stop,
leaving me focused, centered as a top—
amazed to find the fields of stars so near,
campestral silences less frightening.

AT FRESH POND PLAZA

Cars eddy in the rotary.
I park. Windows bead, streak, and drain.
At long last the portiere of rain
divides; you surface close to me,

for once real water on your coat,
wild eyes, as always, submarine.
Where can we go—gamin, gamine,
chilled, spiking, buttoned to the throat,

trembling right now to be alone?
Void stockroom in the depths of Zayre...
Come on. A rippling lifts our hair,
starts seiche-like cranking, bone on bone.

DAYBREAK
(after Baudelaire)

Reveille rasps across the barrack's square,
and sashes rattle, jarred by gusts of air;
bleak hour when dreams beleaguer teenage heads,
torturing horny boys to hump damp beds.
The feeble lamp that ogled me all night
dissolves into the sky, the tidal light
sweeping it eastward—as I watch it drown
my shipwrecked spirit founders and goes down.
Breezes rise, people rise for the rat race;
cold air is tingling like a drying face;
some tire of words, others of making love.
Here and there wisps of smoke appear above
sharp roofs. Johns serviced, shoeshine boy or veep,
whores suck in the raw opium of sleep.
The homeless gather where an oil drum stands,
get a fire going, blow on frozen hands.
The hour when city hospitals entomb
women in labor in an ashen gloom
that multiplies their pain. A cock far off
rachets up bloody sputum, cough by cough.
A flood of fog has set whole blocks afloat.
The dying die—a rattle in the throat,
and then the gurney, laundry, pails and swabs.
Hustlers head in, exhausted by their jobs.
Shivering in her hues of pink and green,
the dawn proceeds along the prostrate Seine;
and diehard Paris rubs blear eyes and turns
to traffic in his urinals and urns.

ANSWERING MACHINE

Scared sick you'd call it off, I grew to be
as strung-out on the messages you'd leave
as you on those blue pills that got you free.

Reaching my winter rental on the bay
alone at night, I'd conjure a reprieve
by climbing the dark staircase the same way,

and (as though terms were spells) "triangulate":
I'd gaze—call indicator out of sight,
consciously breathing—seaward through the plate

glass till the blood that juddered in my head
calmed to far pulses from the Cleveland Light,
then sideways…fixed on what I hoped flashed red.

EXTRACTION

I'd queasily been seated in the so-called
   dental island for more than half an hour
   since the technician had ducked out with X rays—
a hollow pulp-sick throb insistent in
   a lower molar—when the dentist entered.
   (I'd picked his ad out of the Yellow Pages
that morning because he took MasterCard
   and walk-ins on an emergency basis.)
   "I'm Doctor Milligan," he mumbled as
he sidled up, not meeting my eyes. "Sorry
   I've got to." He took a gauze pad and caught
   the tip of my tongue between fat palps, pulling
up, down, one way, another, reaching back
   to aim the high-intensity reflector
   into my mouth. Finally he let go,
and, almost as an afterthought, damp boneless
   hands braided my neck, clavicle to jaw.
   "You don't have oral cancer," he said. "See it
in all ages, recently had to tell
   someone, ruined my week. If I had cancer,
   I'd throw it in." Holy shit, what's all this?
Why was—but gums were numbing and the needle
   went in, sliver of glass in orangeade,
   and he was flapping my cheek and assuring
me that the chance of anaphylactic shock
   was receding because I wasn't turning
   blue, and we could proceed to the curettes,
mouth ratchets, burrs, and mandibular forceps
   required for the extraction. Afterwards
   while I reluctantly focused a mirror
on flesh-prongs clutching bloody gel, he said
   he'd left med school so as not to deliver
   news any more dire than a root canal—
Enough. Presented with a growing panic
   I got out of there fast, praying my mouth
   would keep affirming his career decision.

Tattoo

Then as the artist leaned to needle in
your true love's flash (flower, hummingbird), inked tip
quick as its wing beat puncturing the skin,

though I was just the "lover on the side"
our hands still fused in one white-knuckled grip,
the moment that your flesh was modified.

CASTAWAY

After you'd left me all at sea
I jerked off till I bled,
lifesaving strokes of therapy
whose wake of theta waves let me rehearse
and launch what could be said
in hand-blown bottles (like this verse).

Cigarettes, coffee, cortisone,
the stores were running low;
I wrote my fingers to the bone
determined if you couldn't understand
or care you'd damn well know
how salt the nausea, far the land.

Now strung out nerve cords tangle, knot,
and tighten, biting back
into themselves, their own garotte;
squeeze strength from flesh obsession flensed and thinned.
Body and mind go slack.
—Listen. I'm whistling for a wind.

SONG FOR AN OLD MATTRESS

I'm sorry that our comforter
keeps oozing batting, silly goose,
like us she's suffered much abuse;
her brilliant flowers—white, red and gold,
grizzled to shades of what they were;
the rotten threads no longer hold,
we shouldn't be too hard on her.

Why women go? Well, Al, no doubt,
was hung, Beth rich, Carl cute, Dan spaced,
Ed's smegma had a sweeter taste,
enough. Third parties play a role
but when the other's factored out
so much remains we can't control,
know, or do anything about.

Your ticking reeks, your frame is shot,
your springs are going, one by one,
I'm sleeping with a skeleton
secretions greased and jism stained;
yet you've forgiven and forgot,
accepted me, never complained,
were always there when they were not.

OLYMPIA MARKET, NEW BEDFORD

August. A hectic freshness touched with rot
stalls in the storefront. Amber half-lights flit
through plastic shades to strips of flypaper
above raw duckboard flooring. Lettuce rusts.
Boxes puff dust. Peaches congeal with green
excelsior. Dateless cans linger past
their shelf life's twilight. Groceries aren't sold
elsewhere downtown. A carless clientele—
no longer mainly black, Cape Verdean,
or Portuguese, some clutching food stamps—waits
for one register, wooden cigarette
rack from the '50s jammed on top; a slat
shields figures coyly like the eye-bar scanned
in *Confidential* or *Police Gazette*.
Buying some (I hope) not quite blinky milk,
I think of a hot Sunday in New York
years ago, subway platform empty save
for a stained man in Nedick's coveralls
and oddly military paper hat
on duty at his counter, and a voice
inside me saying "you'll end up like that,"
then as right now fear breaking out like sweat.

SHAVE

I look into the mirror, I'm not there,
beneath the beard I can't quite find my face,
one of these days I won't be anywhere.

Features emerging from the lather bear
some slight resemblance...really just a trace...
I look into the mirror, I'm not there,

this raw retrieval stored inside tough hair
insisting vis-à-vis the data base
one of these days I won't be anywhere—

take sex, for starters. The appraising stare
dismisses flesh that's slipping from its place;
I look into the mirror, I'm not there,

half-glimpsed Cyrillic barroom labels share
in some pier glass the next blink will erase;
one of these days I won't be anywhere.

For now the straight razor that laid this bare
will stay locked in the worn pile of its case;
I look into the mirror, I'm not there,
one of these days I won't be anywhere.

CHEAP DATE

Such times as I'd drop by
you'd lead me to the den
straight past your parents, who'd
pointedly sit there glued
to talk shows, CNN,
the volume turned up high.

So what if dystrophy
shriveled your tits and clit
as long as you'd crouch, eyes
famished, between my thighs;
I treated you like shit,
your only hold on me

exerted on my twists
and turnings in the chair;
then as I'd start to come
your rage at being numb
pinned me exploding there,
gripped as with cuffs on wrists.

WAKE UP CALL

Weak light. An itchy trickling.
Fingertips spring to my face
and then back as if scalded.
Bleeding again—that same mole—

Earth tilts and my spine is pressed
against the coldest pace, pole
of cold, Verkhoyansk of fear.
Later, I cower under

paper sheets as the doctor
turns the Halogen Cool Spot
on...slowly as a spider
one mote lowers in its beam.

BEHOLDERS

We used to stargaze, laid back in your yard,
serenely vigilant on summer nights.
How happily myopic we'd become,
tracking the planets, planes, and satellites
within our private planetarium—
such total disregard
for clustered asterisks that mark the place
where lovers, say, two thousand years ago
must surely have spelled out *Epsilon, Rho,*
Omega, Sigma, blind as the god's face.

You left with help from Prozac, feeling blah,
but called weeks later: could we go to bed
just once more?...some dysfunction and so on...
then thanked me after thigh highs laced my head.
I noticed a new seascape: so—you'd gone
to see the Delacroix
exhibit by yourself. Put on the spot,
you offered me the print, not meaning to.
Its whitecaps, mere notations, dot dark blue;
I've time now to connect them, better not.

TRIP

Last August I drove up to Burlington
to talk to you. She'd left a year ago
but still I couldn't sleep. If anyone,

I thought, knew how to help me, you would know.
My consciousness felt shaky, ill-defined.
As we sat smoking on the portico

of the Ethan Allen House, I had some kind
of out-of-body sense I can't explain—
becoming carbonated comes to mind—

I seemed to fizz, charged particles of pain,
then wick away into the blue abyss
glimpsed through the cirrus over Lake Champlain.

Fatigue, rare cigarette, the cause of this?

BANK

Iron dialectic
of deposit and withdrawal;
wage earners await the summons to approach
inside velvet ropes.

Out in the hall the brass
shoe-polishing stand looms larger than life,
pharaoh's throne with massive arms, footrests,
a kneeling supplicant's worn, uplifted palms.

Surveys put shining shoes
at the base of the job status pyramid,
some ninety steps below the Supreme Court Bench,
its statistical antithesis.

Paper of different value rustles together.
Fan vents softly roar like waterfalls
beyond bone-dry arroyos.
A fierce fluorescence beats down.

OVERCOAT

No other lovers counted. Though she said
I've not much left, sweet mingling filled her bed,
   pot, lubricants, the piscine smells of sex;
dewberry, jasmine lingered overhead.

Cold set in. Humming "Be My Number Two,"
he rummaged sorry castoffs, would this do?
   Next day, Salvation Army drab came back
from the dry cleaner's, pattern showing through,

its herringbone cross purposes defined:
parallels/opposites that brought to mind
   some Wheel of Fortune cipher, the life card
(along with "The Magician") fate assigned.

He learned her pop and tarot, rightly seen,
spanned love and loss, all registers between
   those heights Montale called art's second life
and hope's misreading, heartbreak's mondegreen.

Before her flight she e-mailed him a note:
"Keep warm please in your beautiful new coat."
   It's new, dear heart, the way you make me so—
"Make it new?" Right. So he sat down and wrote.

Topos

(after Camões)

Times change, hearts change,
trustlessness, trust;
what's craved now must
seem new and strange.

Memories stain,
hopes go bust;
of joys (joys?)—just
longings remain.

Time turns the year's
dead white to green,
my words to tears—

change, each day seen,
itself appears
a changed routine.